JEREMY RAISON

Jeremy Raison is a writer and director. He was Artistic Director of the Glasgow Citizens Theatre for seven years during which time the company tripled its box office, was nominated for seventy three awards and transferred work to the West End and internationally. He also ran Chester Gateway Theatre for four years for which he won the TMA/ Stage Award for Outstanding Achievement in Regional Theatre.

Other awards and nominations include the Marrakech Film Festival Gold Star, Manchester Evening News Best Touring Production, Liverpool Post and Echo Best Production (twice), BBC Radio 4 Young Playwrights and Plays and Players Best Children's Play Award, Real to Reel Best International Short Film and a CATS Award for Best Production for Children and Young People.

He is the author of more than 30 plays including The Sound of My Voice (Citizens, Assembly), Blitz (Traverse), Charlie and the Chocolate Factory (Sadlers Wells, Dominion West End, national touring), Don Juan (Citizens), Heart and Soul (Chester Gateway), Wake Me In the Morning (Oran Mor), Jumping Jack Flash (Liverpool Everyman), Savage Britannia (National Theatre Studio, Mandela), A Distant Shore (National Theatre Studio) and A Child of Europe (Theatre Workshop). He has also written extensively for radio/audio: Music To See By, Cuckoo, The Readers of Broken Wheel Recommend, Eavesdropper (all R4), Sam's Secret Orchestra (R3) and a six hour WW1 Project for Amazon Audible. For film he wrote and directed Seen for BBC 1.

ALSO BY JEREMY RAISON

Wake Me In the Morning
Candyland
Bring Me Sunshine
Therese Raquin adapted from Emile Zola
The Sound of My Voice adapted from Ron Butlin
Heart and Soul a drama with live soul music

THE RAIN GATHERING

by

Jeremy Raison

I3 PUBLISHING

First published by 13 Publishing in Great Britain, 2014

The Rain Gathering copyright © Jeremy Raison 2014

Jeremy Raison has asserted his right to be identified as the author of this work

ISBN 978-1-909809-09-3

A CIP catalogue record for this book is available from the British Library

Cover photograph © Jeremy Raison

For information on the author: www.jeremyraison.com

The Rain Gathering was first performed in November 1987 at the National Theatre Studio. The cast was as follows:

HIM Ralph Fiennes
HER Lizzy McInnerny

Director Jeremy Raison
Music/soundscape Jonathan Whitehead

The play was subsequently presented in February 1988 at the National's Cottesloe Theatre:

HIM Ralph Fiennes
HER Lizzy McInnerny

Director Jeremy Raison
Music/soundscape Jonathan Whitehead
Designer Alison Chitty
Lighting Mark Seaman

A further production was mounted at the Traverse Theatre in July 1988 and ran during the Edinburgh Festival:

HIM Ben Daniels
HER Geraldine Fitzgerald

Director Jeremy Raison
Music/soundscape Jonathan Whitehead
Designer Emma Fowler
Lighting George Tarbuck

A version was broadcast on radio as part of the inaugural Radio 4 Young Playwrights Festival in October 1988 directed by Jeremy Mortimer.

CAST

HIM
HER

Both in their 20s

SETTING

The play is set on a beach and a variety of locations.
The original production used a soundscape. It also
benefited from being played in a large space. Staging
should be fluid and continuous.

ONE

HIM He sees his grandfather still sitting exactly where he always sat when he wanted to be alone, in his chair by the fire, brooding. He knocks on the door, but his grandfather doesn't hear. He knocks louder and enters this room which he's hardly ever entered in twenty five years of Christmas and Easter visits, which he's only entering now... It takes a while for his eyes to become accustomed to the gloom. His grandfather is staring at the fire, watching the last embers glow. The fire's nearly out, but the electric lights are off. "Do you want the lights on, Grandpa?" The old man doesn't hear. The room is growing cold, his grandfather is beginning to notice a chill. Still he hasn't sensed the younger man's presence; he continues staring, staring, his face blank in the shadows of this dying firelight. His grandson has remained with his hand on the door knob, unsure whether to step into the room or to go now and come back.

THE SOUNDS OF A BEACH BEGIN TO FADE UP: WAVES, WIND AND GULLS.

HIM His grandfather begins to search for the blanket which has fallen off his knees, and soon, looking round the study, he will notice the younger man in the doorway. "I came to say goodbye," says the young man for the last time.

TWO

THE SOUND OF A LOUD CRASHING WAVE, THEN THE NOISE FADES TO BACKGROUND BEACH.

HER They're on a beach.
HIM There's sand in his shoes.
HER She's in bare feet.
HIM He wants to sit down.
HER She wants to wander. She's restless today.
HIM Like a caged horse. One of her moods. She's always been moody.
HER Today she won't settle at all. She'll hardly answer his questions.
HIM His attempts at conversation are pointless. He doesn't know what to say.
HER She's not listening.
HIM She won't listen. Why has she brought him out here, from the church? He has a sudden desire to make her laugh. To see her smile.
HER She won't respond. She refuses.
HIM He wants to slap her. No, how can he even think like that? But do something. He does nothing. Wonders what she is thinking, supposes her to be thinking of the two of them, supposes -
HER She says nothing
HIM They both say nothing.

THE SOUNDS OF THE BEACH ARE NOW VERY QUIET.

HIM In the silence he can hear the waves and the wind and the gulls.

THREE

THE BEACH FADES. A BAR.

HIM Are you -?

Or

Um - excuse me - ?

Or

Claire? It's good to meet you. I thought I wouldn't recognise you.

Or

I'm sorry, I was worried I was going to be late -

Or

I hope you've not been waiting long.

Or

Do you want a -

Or

Shall we just - ?

Or

HER What's your poison?

HIM No, I'm buying these.

Or

HER No, I don't drink at lunchtime.

HIM Or

Where shall we sit? You do want to sit down?

HER We're not exactly spoilt for choice, are we, chuck? It's hardly des res in here. Mind you, I haven't got long.

HIM Or

HER Let's park ourselves, shall we? Any particular piece of parquet? My car's on a double yellow.

HIM Or

HER So how much are you paying?

HIM Or

It's good to meet you, I'm Jamie.
HER Course you are, pet, I'm Claire.

FOUR

LATER, IN THE BAR.

HIM I thought I'd lost you.

HER I nearly didn't come. I was trying to talk myself out of it. But when I heard your plaintive little voice on the phone, I thought, God, this guy's in panic, I've got to get in there and calm him down.

HIM You don't seem very keen.

HER Would you be, in my shoes?

HIM I could look for someone else. If that's better -

HER You won't find anyone else, will you? I mean, what are you paying? Peanuts. I'm not blaming you. It's not your money, is it? Oh, God, money, did I say money? Don't remind me.

HIM I couldn't imagine what you'd look like. Over the phone.

HER Well, I nearly didn't make it, did I? I've been in bed for a week with a stinking cold. We had to drive up in the pouring rain, overnight. Water was gushing in through the roof, we had Kleenex all over the dashboard - have you got a tissue? No wonder I'm sniffing. Christ, I'm dying for a fag.

HIM I'm sorry, I don't smoke.

HER I'm giving up anyway. Is your hair naturally that colour? God, I feel ill.

HIM If you want to see the space, I can fix a visit. If you still want to do it?

HER You don't have anyone else. Nobody local anyway. Nobody who'd do it for the pittance you're offering. No, I've given you my word, pet, I've said I'll do it, I wouldn't let you down.

HIM I could call later to confirm a time?

HER I'll be out.
HIM You don't have an answerphone?
HER God, I'd die for an answerphone. Listen, I have to go.

FIVE

IN HIS MIND: THE SOUND OF A PROJECTOR WHIRRING.

HIM His mind replays everything that's happened. Like a film full of quick cuts.
HER Cut.
HIM That night.
HER Cut.
HIM The hospital.
HER Cut.
HIM This beach.
HER Cut.
HIM The funeral.
HER Cut. Cut.
HIM His mind won't stop turning.
HER Cut.
HIM Turning things over.
HER Cut.
HIM Words.
HER Cut.
HIM Words.
HER I think you should go.
HIM Cut.
HER I'm so sorry.
HIM Cut.
HER I'm so sorry. I wouldn't have hurt you for the world.

SIX

A LARGE EMPTY HALL AT NIGHT. AN ECHOING, HOLLOW SPACE.

HIM Hi.

HER Oh! It's you! You surprised me.

HIM I'm sorry, I didn't mean -

HER Doesn't matter. What are you doing here anyway? Sneaking in for a quick peek, are we?

HIM I just came to lock up. That's all. Maybe I should come back?

HER Nearly finished. What time is it, anyway?

HIM Half eleven.

HER You're joking! It was three o'clock only half an hour ago.

BEAT.

HIM I won't talk if you're concentrating.

BEAT.

HIM How's everything going then? Good?

HER Fine. If you like slaving away all day over bits of material and thread.

HE DOESN'T LEAVE.

HER Oh, go on, then, cop a hold of this, would you?

SHE OFFERS HIM A TAPE MEASURE.

HER And you can tell someone it's a bit parky in here. I mean, I do have blood. Even if it's not royal.

HIM Sorry?

HER Don't worry, it's not your fault, is it?

HIM They run the heating from somewhere down south. By remote control. I'll speak to them -

HER They know the temperature's different up here, do they?

HIM I'll see what I can do.

HE'S NOT SURE WHAT TO DO WITH THE TAPE MEASURE.

HIM Where do you want it? I don't know if I can reach.

HER Story of my life. I finally get a man in and he's useless. Don't worry, it doesn't need to be exact, just chuck it up as near as you can and hope for the best. That's my motto, anyway! What colour would you like?

HIM I don't know.

HER I am allowed to paint? I mean, this place is a dump, pardon my French, who's going to mind if I tart it up un peu?

HIM Well, I don't -

HER You're the wrong person to ask. Don't mean to sound rude. They should be delighted I've done all the hard work for them.

HIM I'll have to check first. OK? See what they allow and don't allow.

HER Oh, God, it'll be long knocked down by then. Don't panic, I'm joking, aren't I?

BEAT.

HIM There's a party. After. On Sunday night. I don't know

if - has anyone told you? I thought I should say - in case no one else has. Do you think you'll be going?
HER I have to be up early, I've a lot of work on. Here, hold this end, would you?

SHE GIVES HIM THE TAPE MEASURE AGAIN.

HIM You needn't stay long.
HER I'd like to go, I never go partying. But I've another job on, haven't I? I'm a week behind, it's quite a drive.
HIM You'll be exhausted.
HER Some of us need the money.
HIM Yes.
HER What's that supposed to mean?
HIM You said.
HER Me and my big mouth, eh?

BEAT.

HIM Do you move around much?
HER Wherever the work is. Everywhere but here. Actually working at home, forget it. Can't afford to be choosy. Not when you're me. I'm doing this for four hundred. I mean, I must have been mad. You wouldn't know if I'm allowed to use screws?
HIM I'll find out tomorrow.
HER Don't worry, you don't have to look after me.
HIM We're meeting tomorrow. The committee -
HER The great and the good. They'll hardly notice, will they? If I gouge a bit here and whack in a few nails there. What else? No, I think that's it for now.
HIM If you have any problems, just give me a call. You don't want a drink?
HER God, are you always this fresh? I need my bed.

HIM You back in tomorrow?

HER I'm away tomorrow.

HIM There's only three days to go.

HER Doesn't time fly when you're having fun? Don't worry, chuck, I'll throw something together.

HIM I really can't tempt you?

HER I'm going home! Do you need a lift?

HIM I'm on my bike.

HER So where's the leather?

HIM Push bike.

HER Sweet. I hope you've a helmet and plenty of day-glo.

HIM You can't park a car. Not in this city.

HER Don't tell me. I saw sixteen traffic wardens all standing in one doorway.

HIM Today?

HER No, I've been in here, haven't I? I bet you're a vegetarian.

HIM I like eating fish.

HER That's why you have thighs. Now I haven't left anything… ?

HIM If there's anything else…

SEVEN

HER She felt so stupid going to the funeral. They looked at her as if she'd just landed from Mars. He'd got this huge extended family, she hadn't met any of them, he had great aunts coming out of the woodwork. One old boy looked as if he was about to produce an ear trumpet at any moment. They were all drinking sherry and eating asparagus sandwiches. The house was big and rambling, there were tarpaulins all over the roof. The walls were peeling, there was this peculiar smell of damp. It was like Psycho and bloody freezing to boot. One fire lit in the whole house, dogs all over the place, dog hairs everywhere, she wondered why they couldn't just have central heating like normal folk. One of his sisters attempted conversation, she was dressed head to toe in Harvey Nicholls. 'Oh, so you're James' girlfriend, are you, he's talked a lot about you.' She felt like saying, 'Actually, no, I'm just his ex-fuck.' That would give them something to talk about. The whole time she was there she ached to be gone.

EIGHT

THE BEACH FADES BACK IN, A SURGE FOLLOWED
BY QUIETER BACKGROUND.

HIM (distant) Claire. (close) Claire, I -
HER It's a mistake, she should never have come.
HIM He has to say something. There used to be a town here.
HER What?
HIM Thousands of houses. It was a major port. It was very
prosperous: nearly as big as London until a storm swept it all
away in the thirteenth century. I was reading about it. They
had a huge church. The only thing left now is one gravestone
- his grandfather's grave had no gravestone, they said it
wasn't ready. The sea washed everything else away. The last
thing to fall was the church steeple, on some nights you're
supposed to hear the bells tolling under the water.
HER She's only half listening, she just wants to go home
HIM It comes inland at a rate of four inches a year, they
reckon it's come in over a mile since Roman times, they
can't do anything to stop it.
HER They could have stood further back.
HIM Mmm?
HER They didn't need to build here, did they?
HIM They built by a river, it got silted up; there were
marshes behind, they couldn't move back, they were
trapped.
HER They should have built on concrete.

BEAT.

HIM Claire -
HER My father worked at a nuclear plant like this.

18

HIM I know.

HER I went round it with him once, he had a special phone in case of emergencies. He was supposed to be the first one called out if anything terrible happened.

HIM He knows.

HER She thinks of her father, how he invented his own language, how he used to play concertos on his hands by squeezing the air. And he used to sing her lullabies, they had strange words: "Go to sleep, my Zibsie/Go to sleep, my pet/ Go to sleep, my Zibsie/ Or I'll kick you in the head!"

HIM When we were children we used to play here, on the beach. No matter the weather. Come rain, wind or shine, we were outside.

HER She's thinking of her mother.

HIM We'd walk the dogs over here.

HER How she's always been a disappointment to her.

HIM Fly kites if there was a bit of wind.

HER Two grand pianos in the house and she still complained.

HIM There was no power station then.

HER Kicked and screamed to get away.

HIM It's only been built in the last twenty years.

HER Shouted that she never wanted to practice again!

HIM At night it's lit up like some gigantic fairy tale castle.

HER Never wanted to go near a bloody piano again as long as she lived. She thinks of her mother in her flat on her own.

HIM We used to see how long you could stand in front of the waves before the water covered your boots! I wouldn't swim here now. Even though the sea's warmer than it used to be. And they say the control rods are made of the wrong material.

HER She thinks of her mother in her flat on her own.

HIM They'd be the first thing to melt if there was a problem and they're meant to be the last!

HER She knows her mum's better off without her father.

HIM They held an enquiry, it lasted three years.

HER But what it must have meant to her when Harry died.

HIM It produced nothing.

HER Harry had been her friend for years. He's asked her to marry him many times, she's always turned him down.

NINE

HE'S ON THE PHONE. A NUMBER OF DIFFERENT PHONE CONVERSATIONS.

HIM I'm sorry for calling.

HIM I wanted to speak to you.

HIM I'd like to see you very much.

HIM Claire, you must know by now, I mean, I do like you very much.

HIM Someone told me you were living with somebody, is that true?

HIM Oh God, tell me if I'm making a complete fool of myself.

TEN

A SERIES OF PHONE CALLS. THE TONE OF EACH CAN BE DIFFERENT.

HER Look, yes, I'm thinking of getting married to someone.

HER No, I'm not living with him, he doesn't live here.

HER I really don't like talking about my private life.

HER I like you very much. You're very nice, Jamie, you're sweet. I like lots of people I work with, that doesn't mean I want to involve them in my private relationships.

HER I'm not available. People assume - his name isn't important - people assume, if you're involved, if you're not involved.

HER I had a feeling this was going to happen.

HER I told you, I meet lots of nice people.

HER I mean, I'm flattered you like me. If it's going to be difficult for you - Really I am.

HER I don't feel that way about you, I'm sorry. It would be nice just to be friends.

HER I don't feel romantically inclined.

HER It can't be anything else, that's all it can be.

HIM To touch her.
To hold her.
In his arms.
To feel the warmth of her.
To feel her body against his. Against him.
The fold of her.
To hold her.
To hold her.
To hold.

ELEVEN

THEY'RE BACK ON THE BEACH. A LIGHT DRIZZLE.

HIM It's beginning to rain.

HER He's obsessed by the rain, by the never ending shaping of his days and his moods by the rain outside, by the light outside.

HIM It's drizzling. You know the Scots have about nine hundred words for rain! Smirr's my favourite. And dreich. Drookit! Raining stair rods. Pelters.

HER She's not sure now why she's come here, what she felt meeting his family for the first time.

HIM Are you sure you're not cold?

HER He was late, she had to wait in the car, they were all looking at her. She kept expecting him to arrive at any moment.

HIM That's the East coast for you. Winds courtesy of Siberia.

HER It's a long way from Turkey, one of his aunts said.

HIM Shall we go back to the house?

HER She watches the rain tap dance clumsily on the waves.

BEAT.

HIM The rain's getting heavier, isn't it?

HER You're always talking about the rain.

HIM I'm sorry, I didn't mean -

HER Where else can we go?

HIM We can't talk at home, there's too many people.

HER You know they thought you'd never get here at all?

HIM The train was delayed. I never even had time to change properly, to wash. I felt - And he looks at her, her hair becoming wet in this rain, her eyes, the mascara's run, her eyes.

HER She thought seeing him again would be easier than it is.

HIM Why did you come?

HER Suddenly she can't bear him to be near her, she has an overpowering desire to run.

HIM How are you? Are you OK? Really? Is everything - ?

HER She stops herself from fleeing, forces herself to face him in the rain. Fine, I'm fine, Jamie. I'm fine.

HIM You look tired.

HER Well I was up all night driving, wasn't I?

HIM They stand in the rain, unspeaking, the brutal winter waves crashing round them, the sky flat grey -

HER I'm sorry about your grandfather.

BEAT.

HIM Why did you come?

TWELVE

HIM She was supposed to be marrying someone else. That was one of the first things she said to me. They should have been married two months before, they'd just found themselves in different places, that's what she said. They'd planned to move, she said, he'd gone, she was to join him when the job was over, she said. That what she'd said to him. That's what she said to me.

HER She didn't know if she wanted to be married anyway. It was her mother and sister wanted her to be married, she was in no hurry. But she should have been married already.

THIRTEEN

LYING ON A LAWN.

HIM Last summer I went to this place called Torcello. It's across the marshes from Venice, you have to get up really early, the sea was all misty, you go in a little motor boat with a guide, it felt like we were going back into an old world, you seem to go for hours and hours through the reeds. I've no idea how they find their way. Then you come to Torcello itself. And it's incredible. The sun is rising. And all you can see is water, the marshes. And this huge cathedral. It's the only building in sight. A massive cathedral in the middle of the marshes, just - floating. It's extraordinary. It seems to be built on water.

HER Do you know Stuart's never been abroad. He's never been in a plane. Mind you, I haven't been out of Britain much. I've been to Greece. Oh, and I've been to Spain. But that's about it. I'd love to go abroad. I'd love to go travelling. I'd love to go to Venice.

HIM Has he really never been in a plane?

HER No. I keep telling him to go.

HIM Doesn't he want to?

HER He's never really had the chance, I suppose.

FOURTEEN

SHE'S ON THE PHONE TO HER FIANCE. HE'S SPEAKING ON A NUMBER OF OCCASIONS.

HER I know, Stuart. But -

HIM I can't tempt you to another drink?

HER I know I said I would be back down. But - I can't. Not yet. It's a job, it's money.

HIM Or do you want to have lunch again tomorrow?

HER I've been busy. But what have you been up to?

HIM Or there's a good film on tonight.

HER Oh I know but things came up. There's a possibility of another job. I've been having meetings.

HIM Or you could come round to my flat for supper, everyone's out.

HER I don't know. I'll let you know.

FIFTEEN

HER Well, we were having fun. It was enjoyable. He made me laugh. I was lonely, I suppose, I don't know. I mean, I hadn't been on my own for two years, it hadn't been easy, Stuart never had any money, I was supporting him, it was an enormous drain then. I didn't work for ages. I was in love, I suppose. God, love: men always bring me bad luck. It was a sort of relief, him going away, down South. Love is so time consuming. You feel responsible. You worry all the time. I don't want to be responsible for someone else. I don't know. Things hadn't been going too well, we hadn't made love for ages, I mean, I'm not a very sexy person. My flat's freezing, we used to sleep in long johns, pyjamas, three jumpers, socks, scarves. I even wore a balaclava, it was like liking inside an iceberg.

SIXTEEN

HER They're in her car. It's warm. She thinks about her empty flat. The iceberg. I must go.

HIM I've had a nice evening.

HER It's your money. If you've got it, flaunt it, that's what I say.

HIM They're outside his flat.

HER She's taken him home. Again.

HIM He's taken to leaving his bike behind. You don't want to come in for coffee?

HER I ought to go back. Why should she go back? There's no one at home.

HIM A nightcap?

HER He still hasn't moved.

HIM Her arm brushes his. What time tomorrow?

HER You can't take me out every night. You'll spend all your inheritance.

HIM I don't mind.

HER Save your cash for a nice girl.

SHE TOUCHES HIS ARM WITH HER HAND.

HER There's plenty of them around. Her flat's cold. Are you going to have coffee?

HIM I don't drink coffee, I'll make you some.

HER You're too healthy for your own good.

HIM If you want coffee. Or tea? The caffeine will keep you awake for the drive back.

HER You think I need caffeine? He's leaning towards her.

HIM If you'd rather have tea.

HER She doesn't want to move.

HIM If you want tea.

HER She doesn't want him to go.
HIM If you'd rather have me.
HER What?
HIM I said you can have tea, if you'd rather.
HER She wants to hold him. She wants him to hold her.

HE HOWLS.

HER You are stupid. What would happen if she kissed him? Would the world change?

HE HOWLS AGAIN LIKE A WOLF.

HIM It's a full moon!
HER God, I want a new car.
HIM I like this one.
HER You can have it, chuck.
HIM Is this the Kleenex you use when it rains?
HER It comes in here. Five hundred quid and it's all yours, mate.
HIM I don't like cars.
HER You're OK, you can afford taxis.
HIM I never take taxis!
HER Too bleeding' right, mate, you're too mean.

BEAT.

HIM I had a car before I came up. I stole it from my parents. Well, they let me have it. I never really asked. It was always breaking down. That's probably why they didn't mind. I used to park it on a steep hill to get it started in the morning. You had to cover the engine at night to stop it getting damp. I used an old cagoule. Well, I'm not sure it was that old. I forgot it was on once and the cover got caught in the fan belt when I was driving on the motorway. The engine was screaming. I was in the fast lane and had to pull over onto the hard shoulder with a dead car. I thought I was going to die.

HER He leans his head on her shoulder.

HIM It's nothing serious.

HER He turns his face to look at her.

HIM He likes being her friend.

HER She can feel his breath on her face. Haven't you got long eyelashes?

HIM She's different.

HER He's so gentle. So soft. Like a lamb to the slaughter.

HIM He knows she's engaged.

HER The cold's beginning to come through the cracks in the roof.

SEVENTEEN

HER FLAT'S BEEN BURGLED.

HIM Christ, what a mess. What have they taken? What were they looking for?
HER I don't know why they chose my flat.
HIM The door needs mending. Have you called anyone?
HER Nobody heard them. There was no one there.
HIM I'll find a number. I suppose it's a locksmith. Do you know a number?
HER There's nothing worth stealing.
HIM Why did you call me?
HER I knew you'd be in.
HIM I was just going to bed when you rang.
HER Christ, what a mess.
HIM I'll help you clear up. Unless you want to wait til the morning. There's nobody answering.
HER Why my flat?
HIM I'll try in the morning. What have they taken?
HER The telly. Can't see what else.
HIM You called the police?
HER They said they'll be round. There was nothing worth taking, the telly was rented.
HIM When are they coming?
HER I'm on the ground floor.
HIM I'll make you some coffee.
HER They couldn't say when. I forgot to get milk.
HIM Shall I clear up the mess?
HER The police said to leave it.
HIM We should cover the door. Why don't you sleep?
HER I can't sleep.
HIM You won't get it mended tonight.

HER Would you mind staying?

HIM I can sleep down here. If you have any blankets. I can sleep on the sofa. I'll be your guard dog.

HER You can't sleep on the sofa, it'll be cold in here.

HIM You need someone with you, the door's off its hinges. I'll be fine with more blankets.

HER I don't have more blankets. I'm sure you'll be cold. If you don't feel like staying... You'll die of pneumonia.

SHE'S CRYING. HE GOES TO COMFORT HER.

HIM I won't be cold. I'll stay if you want.

EIGHTEEN

THE BEACH.

HIM I was away.
HER I know.
HIM I was in Turkey.
HER He wants to hurt her.
HIM I wanted to go. I bought a carpet. By mistake really. The boy wouldn't let me go, he followed me across the main square. He said his father was angry with him. That's what they say. I almost didn't have enough money to get home. I only had cash. I went to Istanbul and Izmir. Bodrum as well. It was great. You'd have liked it -
HER Don't.

BEAT.

HIM I would have rung, I wanted to.
HER She doesn't need this.
HIM I thought I was dying. I went to the doctor.
HER What does he want?
HIM I went to the doctor.
HER Why does she care?
HIM I thought I had heart disease. It was just a trapped nerve. I went on holiday with someone.
HER Good. That's good.
HIM You have to go with someone or you can't get it cheap. It was wonderful to get away. It didn't rain once. She's just someone I met on the last job. It isn't anything, she's just a friend. The food was revolting, we sat on the beach all day eating melons.
HER She's got a lot of work coming up.

HIM We moved around. You travel everywhere by Dolmush, it's a kind of local minibus. It's so cheap.

HER She's booked up until May next year.

HIM We had a good time. You'd like her.

HER If she can just keep working, she'll clear her overdraft by Christmas.

HIM I bought you some Turkish Delight. I didn't know when I was going to give it to you. The people there are very friendly, I sat on the back of one bus and they all shared their food with me. Only it was all meat.

HER Did I tell you, I'm moving? I found a cottage in the countryside. Twenty miles drive from town. Only sixty pounds a month on my own.

HIM I missed you.

HER Who is she? Who is she? Who is she?

HIM No one you'd know.

NINETEEN

THEY'RE IN A RESTAURANT, ENJOYING
THEMSELVES.

HIM He's obsessed by dust. He lies on his own and collects
dust. All kinds of different types which he puts in jars and
then labels. The collections' continually growing and he
needs to find ever more different types of dust, he looks for
it everywhere.

HER You've told me this story before.

HIM No, I haven't.

HER Yes, you have.

HIM What happens then?

HER He collects it off girls' jerseys. It's pervy.

HIM You've read the book.

HER You told me.

HIM I don't remember telling you.

HER It must be love. Don't sulk, it was a joke.

HIM I'm not sulking.

HER Yes, you are. Go on, tell me anyway.

HIM There's no point now.

HER It doesn't even have a punchline.

HIM It's not supposed to have a punchline. Anyway, it does
- when he becomes famous for the dust and gets on the chat
show and the jars are empty. He's emptied them all. Awe
can't understand why people are so interested, he's thrown
them all away.

HER You sure know how to tell them.

HIM Well, you ruined it.

HER Great ending.

HIM Shall we get the bill?

UP TO NOW THE BANTER HAS BEEN GOOD
NATURED, LIGHT. SUDDENLY THE MOOD
CHANGES.

HER Shall we go to bed?
HIM Mmmm.

TWENTY

HIM We started an affair. She never told him. I began living there. She never told him. He came up just once, I moved out for the weekend, she never told him. He'd lived there two years, he saw all his friends, but nobody told him. He went away, I moved back in, they'd hardly talked and she still hasn't told him. I fell in love, I never told her.

TWENTY ONE

SHE'S IN HER FLAT, ALONE, WRITING.

HER Bank, eighteen hundred. Mum one thousand. Dad five hundred. Phone seventy. Gas forty. Petrol thirteen. Rent six fifty. Electricity sixty. Coat forty. Cashpoint forty. Exhaust fifty bloody seven. Food five.

JAMIE ENTERS

HIM How are you?
HER Tired.
HIM Have you been working hard today?
HER Not especially.
HIM So why are you tired? I couldn't do any work at all today.
HER And I'm sore. What have you been doing to me? Oh, munch my shoulders, would you?
HIM Where do you hurt?
HER Here - mm, that's better. Gently. Right a bit. Left a bit. Up a bit -
HIM Fire!
HER God, I ache. My back's like wood. I need a tree surgeon.
HIM Can you make the weekend?
HER Don't stop.
HIM You're seeing him.
HER Ow.
HIM You can't get out of it? I put off my parents.
HER I wanted to meet them.
HIM I wanted to see you.
HER Don't stop now, it's lovely.

HIM Why don't you put him off?
HER Don't. Don't change your life for me. Don't fall in love with me. And don't put all your eggs in one basket.

TWENTY TWO

HER Nothing was said. He came up just once, we hardly talked. He saw all his friends. I went round to see Jamie, I don't know why, we fell into bed. We hardly talked. When I got back home, he still wasn't there. He came back drunk, and went straight to bed. I followed him later, he was already asleep; then slept in the next morning; when I woke up, he'd gone. He returned in the evening, to say he was leaving. We still hadn't talked. We still hadn't touched. Nothing was said. I'd lived with him two years - he'd been gone six weeks.

TWENTY THREE

HER FLAT, SUNDAY MORNING IN BED.

HER Your turn to get the papers.
HIM I'm asleep.
HER No, you're not.
HIM It's raining!
HER I always get the papers.
HIM You're never here.
HER Oh, go on.
HIM I will if you make the coffee.
HER God, I'm tired.
HIM I did them both last weekend.
HER You're counting, are you? That's romantic. I couldn't sleep at all last night, I could do with a holiday. Why don't you take me on holiday? Oh, go and get the papers, you're here all the time. I never get a lie in. I'll make it up to you. Go on. Please. All the best ones will have gone.
HIM What did your last slave die of?
HER Honestly, you're such a pushover.

LATER.

HIM Here are the papers - and here's your coffee - and I bought some croissants - they're in the oven.
HER Last of the big spenders.
HIM Oh, and I bought you some Polly-filla for your crow's feet.
HER If you're not nice to me, you won't get your surprise. Close your eyes. No peeping. Happy birthday. Da-na! You can open them now.
HIM You bought a cake.

HER I baked a cake. I didn't have enough money to buy a cake.

HIM You made it?

HER What's wrong with it?

HIM It's fine. It looks fine.

HER It's the only cooking I'm ever going to do for you, so you'd better enjoy it, sunshine. What do you think?

HIM Did you sit on it?

SHE HITS HIM.

HIM Ow! OK, shall we have it now? I have to go soon.

HER Oh, you're always working.

HIM I have to go in, I arranged to meet someone.

HER Boy or girl?

BEAT.

HER You need to look out for yourself more. Say no.

HIM Like you do?

HER I wanted to treat you.

HIM I'll be back later.

HER No you won't, you'll be out whooping it up with Miss Whoever she is. I bet she'll buy you a nice birthday present, won't she?

HIM It's work. I'll be back by five.

PAUSE.

HER At least have a bit of cake before you go. Go on, cut it and be careful.

HIM I'm going to make a wish.

HER What are you wishing for?

BEAT.

HIM The knife won't go in.
HER Pull it apart.
HIM I don't want to ruin it.
HER God, you're so feeble.
HIM I can't just destroy it. Perhaps we should save it. Put it in a glass box so we can remember this moment forever.
HER Just tear it apart with your hands!

TWENTY FOUR

THEY'RE ON THE PHONE.

HIM Ring me tomorrow.
HER I've said I'll try.
HIM Promise.
HER I promise.
HIM Tomorrow you'll phone me.
HER I've said I'll try.
HIM Promise again.
HER I have to -
HIM Tomorrow.
HER Tomorrow. I have to go.
HIM Don't go yet, don't go yet, don't go yet, don't -
HER I have to.
HIM Don't go yet, please, please don't go.

PAUSE.

HIM Claire?
HER Yes. What do you want?
HIM Ring me.
HER I will, but I must go now.
HIM Ring me, promise.
HER Please, let me go.
HIM Promise you'll ring me.
HER I will, I'll try.
HIM Promise.
HER I promise. I promise, now go.

TWENTY FIVE

HER FLAT.

HER What you reading?

HIM It's just a book.

HER I can see that, what book?

HIM From Plato to Nato.

HER What's it about?

HIM It's a collection of political philosophy.

HER God, that sounds a bundle of laughs. Any good pictures?

HIM No.

HER Why are you reading that? Is it so you can impress your smart friends at dinner parties?

HIM I wanted to read it.

HER Would I enjoy it?

HIM I don't think so, no.

HER For all you know I could be a world famous political philosopher.

HIM Who was Plato then?

HER It's not fair, you're always reading. I wish I had time to read. I never read books. Perhaps that's what's the matter with me, perhaps if I had time to read. I never have time to think.

TWENTY SIX

LATER

HER I don't know why you want me, I'm haggard, my neck's getting scraggy, anyone got an iron? I'm old, my mother says I should be having babies. I did this modelling once, the guy who was taking the photographs laid the makeup on with a trowel. I kept thinking it was going to fall off my face and I could use it to build a patio, I think he overdid it un peu, am I that ugly? I looked like Cruella da Ville. I must do something about my hair, it's been like this for years. What should I do with my hair? My mother hates it, the last time I saw her she said: before I die, I'd like to see you with a proper haircut. You could wear a hat, she said, that's it, why don't you wear a hat? She meant it. You could do with a bit of a reshape yourself. Let's have a bath and I'll cut your hair.
HIM I don't want a haircut.
HER You'd look much better. Go on, why don't you run the bath? And tomorrow we'll get you some proper clothes.

LATER

HER I can't pay more bills. The phone bill's over a hundred quid.
HIM You should try not using it at peak rate.
HER I don't use the phone that much.
HIM Then you should have it checked.
HER I've never been charged more than seventy before. I've hardly been here, I've been away working. I saw a car yesterday.
HIM You've got a car.

HER It's too cold. I want something that doesn't leak. Leaky vehicles seem to follow me around. They'll do part exchange. Four hundred.

HIM You've got an overdraft.

HER I've got money coming in at the end of the month. I was furious, the other day, the bank cancelled a cheque for seven pounds. I mean, what's the point? I wish you'd buy a car. Why don't you buy me a car? I wish I had someone to buy me things. I saw some lovely earrings today. I want a washing machine. God, I'm in debt. I wish some of the bastards that owe me money would pay me, I mean they're quick enough to ask for money when I owe them. I've borrowed a grand off my mother which I still owe her. I wish I could pay her back, I mean, let's face it, you don't want your kids scrounging off you when they're old enough to be your parents - when they're middle aged as she tells me. I wish I was rich. It's easy to make money when you've already got money. What's it like to be rich? I wish I was a man.

TWENTY SEVEN

HIM Marry me.
HER You're sweet.
HIM Marry me.
HER It's not real.
HIM Marry me.
HER It's being in love.
HIM Marry me. We've talked about it.
HER You've talked about it.
HIM Marry me.
HER It's not going to last for ever.
HIM Marry me, marry me, please.

TWENTY EIGHT

THE BEACH. THE WIND HAS DIED DOWN.

HIM We could have got married. We could have been married. I would have married you. If you'd wanted marriage. It's not that I didn't offer. It's not that I wouldn't have. It could have happened. It could. If you'd -
HER Jamie, don't.
HIM I wanted to marry you.
HER I said don't.
HIM Are you still seeing him?
HER Which one?
HIM Either. Neither. Someone else, for all I know!
HER You don't want to know.
HIM You still haven't told your fiancé?
HER I'm not going to marry him. Don't ask anymore, Jamie. It'll only make you feel worse.
HIM What can you say that will make me feel worse?
HER Someone said I should have married you. The other day, I was talking about you, they just came out with it -

TWENTY NINE

THEY'RE ON THE PHONE.

HIM I thought you were never going to ring. When are you getting here? You can't get away? It's the weekend. I waited by the phone all week. I thought you were never going to ring me. I wanted to see you, that's all. What's so bad about wanting to see you? Why? Because I'm a pushover? Don't. Don't hang up!

HER Jamie! It's alright, it's alright, it's alright. Stop saying I'm sorry all the time. I can't come down this weekend, no. Look, don't get paranoid on me, just say yes to everything I say, why don't you? What do you mean, no? Jamie! I can't talk now. What do you want, pet? Yes! Yes, me too.

THIRTY

THE BEACH.

HIM The light's fading.
HER We could go and sit in my car.
HIM No.

BEAT.

HER You expect too much.
HIM I never asked you to come here.
HER I never set out to hurt you, Jamie.
HIM It just happened? You just leapt from one bed to another without a second's thought.
HER It wasn't like that.
HIM Just thinking of yourself.
HER It was nothing like that.
HIM No consideration for anyone else.
HER Consideration's a long word.
HIM OK: thought!
HER It did just happen.
HIM Nothing just happens.
HER Do you really want to know how?

PAUSE.

HIM Has anyone told you how selfish you are?
HER Oh, don't be such a martyr.
HIM Only worrying about the next penny.
HER Saint Jamie of the Bleeding Heart.
HIM Where the next fuck's coming from.
HER I'm not your property! I'm no one's property! Get over

yourself! There's a whole world out there.

PAUSE.

HIM Well, I hope you had a good holiday.
HER I had a foul holiday. I don't know who goes to the Costa Brava if they're not Club 18/30? There wasn't space on the beach to lay a towel, you couldn't see the sand, the sun hardly shone. You're meant to be excited because it doesn't rain. Well, the food was revolting. It was melons or nothing. We ended up staying in our grotty hotel room, drinking cheap plonk and watching the cockroaches scurry across the floor.
HIM Well, I'm sorry.
HER I want us to be friends.
HIM Why? Haven't you extracted enough blood? I hurt.
HER Other people hurt too. It's not a death. Thousands of people break up every day.
HIM I don't know what use it is you coming here. It just makes me feel angry.
HER I'm angry too.
HIM You've no right!
HER Why not? I came all this bloody way to see you. To talk to you. Support you.
HIM Support?
HER Oh, why did I bother? I don't know. Do you? Jesus, Jamie, you're so fucking difficult!
HIM Stay!

THIRTY ONE

HER I said I'd only be here for a week.
HIM One more day. I'll be on my own again.
HER Ahhh.
HIM I'll be lonely.
HER I have to go back.
HIM Please.
HER Don't spoil it, it's been lovely. I've got to go. I'll drive you home.
HIM Go tomorrow morning.
HER I'll see you soon.
HIM Don't have a good time, don't fall for anyone.
HER God, I'll be too busy working. Come on, read to me. Educate me, professor.
HIM Only if you promise to stay.
HER Come over here. I can't find the place.
HIM Give it here.

HE READS.

HIM '*Anna Sergeyevna looked at Bazarov for a moment with an expression of utter bewilderment. "But I don't see why it should be impossible to express what is in one's heart."*
"Can you?" asked Bazarov.
"Yes. I can," answered Anna Sergeyevna, after a moment's hesitation.
Bazarov bowed his head. "Then you are more fortunate than I," he replied.
She looked at him questioningly. "As you please, but something tells me that we shall become good friends, I am convinced that your - what shall I call it? - this reserve of

yours will disappear eventually."

Bazarov stood up and moved over to the window. "You'd like to know the reason for this reserve?" he asked.

"Yes," replied Anna Sergeyevna with a flicker of alarm which she did not full understand.

"And you will not be angry?"

"No."

Bazarov stood with his back to her. "Then let me tell you that I love you. Idiotically, madly, with my whole being... There, you've forced it from me."

Anna Sergeyevna held her hands out in front of her. She noticed Bazar's heavy breath misting the window. His whole body trembled.

"Yevgeny Vassilyich," she murmured.

He turned suddenly, crossed the room and seizing both her hands, suddenly drew her to him. She did not free herself immediately; but in another instant had retreated to the corner of the room. "Y-you have misunderstood me," she whispered. Had he taken another step, she felt sure she would have screamed. Bazarov bit his lip and strode out of the room.

Half an hour later, a maid brought Anna Sergeyevna a note from Bazarov, consisting of a single line: " Am I to leave tonight, or may I stay another day?"

HE STOPS READING.

HER Don't stop.
HIM Stay another night. Please? Please - just one -
HER I'll see you when I get back.

THIRTY TWO

HIM She went away, to do a job, she said. She rang from work.
HER She had a problem.
HIM A small problem, that's what she said.
HER She needed help.
HIM That's what she told me.
HER A telephone number was what she wanted.
HIM A telephone number, that's what she said.

THIRTY THREE

HER When I did the test I already knew. I mean, I got up really early and you have to wait an hour and I wouldn't go and look at it, I wouldn't stand and watch it or anything, I just left it there. And there it was clear as daylight. I threw it away. I didn't know it was called the Brook Advisory, and because Directory Enquiries being what they're like in this sodding country, they didn't know either, you'd have thought they - I mean, any normal female I think would probably have heard of the Brook clinic, it was a girl who answered, she had no idea. Well, anyway, I was in a bit of a mess, I was crying a lot, I drove back that afternoon, and I had an appointment the next day. And then they told me I could be part of an experiment. They said you have to be very committed for this, you have to go back nine for ten times, you really shouldn't be on your own, I said there's no way I can do that, I didn't say I'm not committed, I said I couldn't, I was working, I was hardly there, and somehow she managed to rush this hospital appointment. A lot of the problems with things like that is, on the National Health, it's this whole thing they're trying to pass now, this law, eighteen weeks or something, but you know I was very early, I cracked it instantly, I mean I was lucky, I was moved forward two weeks, that makes a hell of a difference, I couldn't have stuck another two weeks, another month would have been normal, it's the first three months where you feel the most changes. I wasn't being violently sick, I was OK, I was getting up and eating ferociously first thing, it seemed to stop it, but your mind's going mad. Your body's saying one thing, your mind's telling you something different. It's sad, really, it should be be of the happiest times of your life.

THIRTY FOUR

HER FLAT.

HIM I thought I'd drop in. You must be tired. I tried to ring first.
HER I've been driving all evening.
HIM I'm wearing your jumper. I wore it all week. I wanted to smell you.
HER It smells of smoke. You've been to a party?
HIM I missed you. I went to one party. How are you? You look tired. I wanted to phone you. I couldn't get hold of you. I did get the job.
HER We can't celebrate. There's no drink in the flat. Why didn't you call first?
HIM I wanted to see you.
HER It's late to be calling. I didn't expect you.
HIM You don't seem too happy.
HER It's one in the morning. I didn't expect you.
HIM I waited all evening. I wanted to see you.
HER You should have rung first.
HIM I did try to ring. You weren't in when I rang.
HER I could have brought wine.
HIM It's too late to buy wine. I thought you'd look different.
HER I was away for a week.
HIM I thought you'd look older. You don't seem happy.
HER I'm tired from the driving.
HIM You don't want to talk?
HER I just want to sleep.
HIM Do you want me to go?
HER No.
HIM What's the matter?
HER I'm sorry - I'm tired.

HIM Tell me. What's wrong?
HER There's nothing wrong. I'm not feeling great.
HIM Shall I get you an aspirin?
HER Just leave me alone!

BEAT.

HER I'm sorry for snapping. Let's go to bed.

THIRTY FIVE

THEY'RE AT A DUCK POND.

HER You're always talking about people you know. Name-dropping these London types. I don't know anyone. I've lived here for years and I never see anyone.

HIM You never go out, that's why. Whenever we go out, you always bump into loads of people.

HER I don't have the money to go out.

HIM You earn more than I do.

HER What's it like to have fun? You're always being invited to parties.

HIM I've been to about one in the last three months.

HER You didn't take me. I'd like to have gone to a party.

HIM Girlfriends weren't invited.

HER That's not what I heard.

HIM What did you hear? You didn't hear anything. There wasn't anything to hear -

HER Then why did you mention it?

HIM I thought you weren't interested.

HER You didn't want me to go, did you?

HIM You'd have made it more fun.

HER Do I embarrass you in front of your posh friends?

HIM Non family weren't invited. You'd have made it more fun.

HER You do say some stupid things.

HIM It's true.

HER I made a dress. I spent the whole day at the sewing machine.

HIM It was a clan gathering. You would have hated it. That Tory minister was there.

HER Is he really as ugly in real life as he is on the telly?

HIM It was a family affair. There were place names.

HER You don't want me to meet your family, do you? Mind you, I'm not surprised, I wouldn't like to meet myself. I'd like to meet your mum. I wanted to meet her when she was up.

HIM You were away.

HER I could have come back.

HIM You were on the other side of the country. I don't know what's so important about meeting my parents. You'll meet them in time. You'd have hated it anyway.

HER I'd like to have gone to a big ball. I suppose a Brass Band in the park's the nearest I'll get. You're really pushing the boat out bringing me here, aren't you? I bet Camilla, or whatever her name is, doesn't get taken to the duck pond. I'm not what you want, am I? There's always some nice girl clinging off you your mother would approve of. Why don't you marry one of them?

HIM There's no one clinging off me.

HER What about that girl you had your arms stuck fast around the other day?

HIM She's a friend.

HER You were holding her tight enough, I thought you were trying to get your prick up her arse.

BEAT.

HIM I've worked with her.

HER You worked with me.

HIM I hadn't seen her for months.

HER You've seen her now.

HIM What's the matter with you, you've been in a mood for days?

THIRTY SIX

HER You remember being wheeled in when you're quite capable of walking, except you might run away screaming, and you lie down, with the nurses in green things looking down, saying, 'Hello, what's your name, what do you do?', sticking a needle in your hand, count to five, zonk. With your legs in the air.

THE HOSPITAL.

HIM She's in hospital. She hasn't yet woken up. He's gone to see her, she's still asleep. He can't see her head at all. She's deep down in the bed. He's sorry for her, sad it's not him. Glad it's not him. If she wakes now, he won't know what to say. He's carrying some flowers, and some fruit and a card. He's terrified. I wish I wasn't here. Suppose she wakes up. If she doesn't, how long will I sit here for? She stirs. Should I kiss her? The nurse brings her tea. He watches her wake, she's wearing no makeup, her face is white.

HER You remember going in, but you never remember coming back.

HIM She's all crumpled, groggy from the anaesthetic.

HER She notices the nurse first, then the tea.

HIM She starts to drink.

HER It takes her a while to notice him. She's thirsty.

HIM Does she want him there, does he embarrass her? He wants to ask her how she is, how she's feeling - what it's... like - but words aren't enough. They can't ever be enough.

HER She knows he's there. She doesn't feel like talking. She's so thirsty. All she wants to do is drink the tea, drink, drink, her throat is parched, why is it so dry?

HIM He doesn't know what to say.

HER She wants another cup of tea. Will the nurse bring another cup of tea?

HIM He has to say something.

HER All she wants is another cup of tea.

HIM He looks round. The nurse has gone. He can't call out. He feels foolish. Everyone must know why he's here. He's out of place in this woman's ward. There aren't many visitors here now. Perhaps people are still at work, what time is it? There are a couple of women with drips in their arms. All he wants is to be alone with her.

HER All she wants is to be alone. To sleep.

HIM She's crying.

HER She feels weepy, soft. She starts to apologise for her tears, she tries to explain. She can't.

HIM He wants to soothe her.

HER Again she starts to say she's sorry. She's still thirsty. So thirsty. She's distracted. She can't stop thinking about the pain. It doesn't go away. It won't go away. She wants to look, to see what they've done to her. The pain. He's far away. She ought to talk to him, he's come to see her.

HIM When will they let you go home?

HER She could say something. But she just wants to go back to sleep. To go deep, deep down inside this bed, in mourning. Please.

THIRTY SEVEN

HER FLAT.

HIM What do you want me to do?
HER Nothing. Whatever you want to do.
HIM What do you mean, whatever I want? What do you want?
HER I've told you. I don't know. Why do you want me, chuck? I'm no good for you. I'm old and hackit. God, change the record, it must be worn out by now. Why don't you find some nice girl with pots of money you can take home to your mother?
HIM I don't want that, I've had that, I was bored stupid.
HER What am I? Am I your bit of rough? Don't you find me boring, pet? God, I bore myself sometimes. Plato has nothing on me.

*

HIM She always cries. Every time we make love now, when we do, she cries. She can't help it, she say, it just happens, she apologises. She asks why is she so stupid, why it's always her? I tell her it's not her fault, theres nothing wrong, she can't expect it to be easy. I don't know whether to stop making love to her, or whether to try and get her through it, how to.

*

HER I've been asked to go to Greece.
HIM Are you going?
HER I was there before. He's invited me to spend the whole

summer.

HIM The one who rings at three in the morning?

HER He doesn't anymore. I'd like to go, I could do with some sun.

HIM What does he want?

HER Exactly.

*

HIM You haven't phoned for ages.

HER I've been busy.

HIM I thought you were coming back on Tuesday.

HER Oh, things came up. There's a possibility of another job. I've been having meetings.

HIM For four days? I thought you'd ring.

HER I wasn't near a phone, I haven't rung anybody.

HIM I asked where you were, no one seemed to know.

HER Ah, you've been spying on me, that's so sweet.

HIM When are you coming home?

HER I'll let you know.

*

HIM When did you get back?

HER Friday.

HIM Why didn't you ring?

HER You're always busy.

HIM I didn't know you were back. I could come round now.

HER I'll be out. I'll see you tomorrow.

HIM I could come round later.

HER I'll be back late.

HIM I thought you never went out.

HER Oh, it's people from work, they're over this evening. I'll see you tomorrow, give me a ring.

*

HER I'm not going to Greece. I've decided. It's more trouble than it's worth.

HIM Good.

HER I've found a cheap holiday in the Costa Brava instead. Oh, it's nothing at all. He's just someone I met on the job. He saw this cheap flight and asked me along. It's stupid really. But if you go with someone, you get it cheap. It isn't anything, he's just a friend. God, did I tell you, there was another bloke there, he was letching all over me, I told him to get knotted, his wife was there too - and their nine month old baby.

HIM When are you going?

HER Oh, I should get out of it really, but he's bought the tickets. Friday. I don't want to hurt anyone. I just need a holiday. He found it, it was the only one I could afford.

HIM You don't want to have an affair with him. The last thing you want is to have an affair with anyone just now, trust me.

THIRTY EIGHT

THE SOUND OF A PROJECTOR WHIRRING AS IN
SCENE FIVE.

HIM Marry me.
HER The smell of you.
HIM Marry me.
HER The feel of you.
HIM Marry me.
HER The breath of you.
HIM Marry me.
HER Everything we said.
HIM Marry me.
HER Everything we did.
HIM Marry me.
HER I care for you.
HIM Marry me.
HER But I'm not coming back.
HIM Marry me.
HER You'd hate me.
HIM Marry me.
HER Don't torment yourself, Jamie.
HIM Marry me.
HER Don't.
HIM Marry me, marry me, marry me, marry me, marry me,
marry me, marry me, marry me, marry me, marry me, marry
me, marry me, marry me, marry me, marry me, marry me,
marry me, marry me -

THIRTY NINE

HIM She told me she was thinking of having an AIDS test. She said she didn't need to do one, they'd have done one anyway when she was in the hospital, wouldn't they? They'd have told her if anything was wrong. She wasn't worried, they'd have to let her know. In the first months we made love all the time. When she was bleeding. All the time.

HER It's Stuart. He used to be an addict.

HIM For Christ's sake, Claire -

HER It's alright, he didn't share needles.

HIM For Christ's sake, do you actually think about anything you do? What is your life, just one big car crash and it doesn't matter who's in the way? Why didn't you tell me?

HER He used to steal them from the laboratory where he worked. It's alright, the hospital would have told me, wouldn't they?

HIM Jesus, you're such an idiot, why didn't you say?

FORTY

HIM She's found a new man, she won't yet admit it.

HER I don't know what I want.

HIM I know it true, you don't always need words.

HER I want a house of my own with a studio for painting in, and a Volvo and money.

HIM There's things you sense, I want to tell her.

HER I'm sick of having an overdraft, I want an adventure, I want passion!

HIM She'll never tell me, she'll start to lie.

HER I don't find him attractive, he's a good friend, that's all.

HIM When I catch her out, she still won't have told me.

HER I don't know why I did it, believe me, I'd never hurt you in a million years.

HIM When I've caught them together, it'll be no surprise.

HER I don't know why. I love you, Jamie.

HIM To cover her tracks, she already tells lies.

FORTY ONE

HER FLAT.

HER I've got something to tell you.
HIM Don't say anything. I'm so angry.
HER I'm sorry.
HIM How could you - ?
HER I'm sorry.
HIM Don't. I'm so fucking - angry!
HER I think you need to go. I'm so sorry.
HIM How could you? After -
HER I'm sorry, you should go.
HIM I hate you.
HER Please.
HIM I hate you, I hate you. I hate you, I hate you I hate you, I hate you. How could you do this to me?
HER Go away!
HIM No!
HER Jamie, stop it!
HIM I'm staying here. Are those his flowers?
HER Yes, he brought them round. I was ill, that's all. It was very sweet of him. Very thoughtful.
HIM You were ill, why didn't you tell me? I'd have come round, you know I would. That's what I'm for.

HE REALISES.

HIM He's here now, isn't it?
HER Jamie.

BEAT.

71

HIM Where is he?

HER Yes.

HIM He's in your bed.

HER Jamie, you're driving me mad. I never meant this -

HIM Don't come near me!

HER I'd never have got through it without you. Jamie.

HIM Don't touch me. Does he even know you've got a fiancé, does he?

HER He's not my fiancé anymore.

HIM And does he know about us?

HER Yes, I had to tell him, you can't not, I mean -

HIM And what, you had a really good laugh, did you?

HER You know it's not like that.

HIM And now you're going on holiday with him, I suppose?

HER Yes.

HIM Why didn't you tell me?

HER Nothing had happened. It only happened -

HIM I don't want to know. Why wouldn't you come on holiday with me? Was it even my baby? I wouldn't be surprised if it -

HER Jamie, no -

HIM Was it?

HER Now don't you start.

HIM Take me home, I'm not staying here…

HER I'm sorry.

HIM (shouts) Have a good holiday!

HER He's not asleep.

HIM He's listening? Has he been listening?

HER I don't know.

HIM Has he had an AIDS test too? (Shouts) Go and have an AIDS test, I won't tell you the result, you can go and sweat it out for yourself -

HER Jamie -

HIM (shouts) I hope the fucking plane crashes.

HER Come on.

HIM (shouts) You do know she's got a fiancé as well? I give it two months, Tops. Get used to it, good luck!

HER Jamie -

HIM Don't you dare touch me! Get your hands off - !

HER I'm sorry -

HIM Just leave me alone!

FORTY TWO

HER He thinks it was easy. That I just moved from one bed to another. Is that what you think? It's hard to be passionate when you've just been in hospital. In bed you're so vulnerable - you feel... you feel at your weakest. The last thing you want is... You can't. It's all connected. It wasn't like that.

GRADUALLY THE BEACH IS FADING UP. IT'S NOT CLEAR IF SHE'S TALKING TO US OR JAMIE.

HER It was a form of escape. I was working away from home, I didn't have any time to myself. When you're away and you meet other people, and you have something in common, it's easy - it's easy to think you have more in common than you actually do. I was so tired. Down. Going through hospital, and then having to go to work. Trying to pretend nothing had happened. I'm sad too. I mean, we were close. It happened at a time when we were probably very close. At a time when I realised -

FORTY THREE

ON THE BEACH.

HIM Do you love him?
HER He's just a friend.
HIM And Stuart?
HER I don't know what he's up to. I used to think he had such wonderful plans. Maybe I expect too much from him. I just think he's wasted. It's a criminal waste of talent. He's not a lab technician. But he doesn't know what else he is. I can talk, I'm as bad I suppose, but at least I struggle from one disaster to another. I don't know what the answer is. I give it a lot of thought, you can't just obliterate the past. But I haven't really missed him. I feel as if I'm in a different league now.
HIM Have you told him yet?
HER About what?
HIM I always thought if I left you alone, you'd tell him. Of your own free will. I thought if I said either Stuart or me, you'd say Stuart.
HER I couldn't bear to hurt him. You don't just stop loving someone, do you?
HIM You never once said you loved me.

PAUSE.

HIM When you went on holiday, I just sat in my room playing records. I don't know how long I sat there. I had this poster on the ceiling, I just stared at it while I played this one record over and over and over and over. I thought about you all the time. I wondered where you were, what you were doing, if you were talking to him, if you were lying in bed with him, if you were curled in his arms, tucked into him, sleeping in his arms.

HER I've seen this Volvo. A friend promised to sell it to me. It's only a thousand. I've been slaving away all year and what have I got to show for it? God, if I had all the money I'm owed, I'd be rich. I bought a ghetto blaster the other day, and a washing machine. I don't know what came over me. I'm still owed £600, I've got £800 coming in from my last job.

PAUSE.

HIM What are you going to do now?

HER I don't know. It's time I moved. I'd move to London if I could afford it. God, I don't know why I live here anymore, I never work here, I'm up and down the motorway like a blue-arsed fly, it's doing my head in.

HIM London's horrible, you won't like it.

HER I should have brought a flat there years ago when I had a regular job. Nobody'll give me a mortgage now. You're lucky. At least you've got a regular job.

HIM I might be leaving too.

HER Oh well, you'll be alright. You always land on your feet, don't you?

HIM I've no idea what to do next.

HER Join the club.

HIM Do you wish you'd had it?

BEAT.

HER How could I? How was I going to bring up a child? Was I going to give up my job? Was I going to move flat? Were you going to be around? Were you going to support us? How could I? I couldn't even look after a dog. I'm all over the place. I can't look after myself. I'm sorry. I'm sorry. I'm sorry I'm sorry I'm sorry I'm sorry. How many times do I have to say I'm sorry before it means anything to you? I am sorry.

FINALLY SHE'S CRYING.

HIM You could have had it.
HER I didn't want it.

FORTY FOUR

HER The story. I think - you can't order things - you can't order - other things come into your mind - I think - other - things things - when you want to - you can't - you can't always - when you want - fragments, moments, memories, fears, death crowd - come into, force into your mind, loom like shadows, spiders' webs, catching you unawares, the shock, whiplash, thought, explosions, ricochets, rebounds.

Start again.

HE STARTS FROM THE BEGINNING, SHE CARRIES ON.

HIM The story. I think - you can't order things - you can't order - other things come into your mind - I think - other - things things - when you want to - you can't - you can't always - when you want - fragments, moments, memories, fears, death crowd - come into, force into your mind, loom like shadows, spiders' webs, catching you unawares, the shock, whiplash, thought, explosions, ricochets, rebounds.

SHE SPEAKS AT THE SAME TIME.

HER To order things, life, events - you can't - things said, things unsaid, world without order, random, painful - in retrospect comes - at the time, life's like - life's like - rubbish scattered on the road, shapeless, dirty, wild - afterwards, looking back - what you see - what you won't see - perceived reality, filtered reality, recollected in tranquillity reality, cold hard reality - I loved him, but.
HIM Love.

BOTH Start again.
HER What am I leaving out?
HIM What am I leaving out?

FORTY FIVE

THE BEACH.

HER They're on a beach.
HIM There's sand in his shoes.
HER She's in bare feet, she's restless today.
HIM Like a caged horse.
HER I think we should go.

BEAT.

HIM He thinks of the graveside. The lowering of the coffin.
HER She knows she won't see him again.
HIM He loves her, this strange contradictory woman, here, now, more than he's ever loved anyone -
HER She loved him. This man. This boy. Once.
HIM One day she'll have a partner and three beautiful children - and two cars. A Volvo for running about town and a 4x4 for taking the kids' surfboards to the beach. She'll live less than forty miles away, but he'll never see her again.
HER She'll see him once. With his wife and child and a dog. A border collie. But he won't see her. It will be fifteen years to the day, but she won't stop and talk. She'll just carry on driving.
HIM This is the last time they'll ever talk.
HER They're so young but this is the last time they'll ever talk. This moment.
HIM You know they built two more reactors. B and C. The second looks like a giant golf ball. Apparently the architect wanted to make it absurdly difficult to build, to delay its progress. Because of his beliefs.
HER She shivers, longs for the odd warmth of her car, the

security of the long, lone drive back to her empty flat. Her fingers are numb.

HIM He thinks of how it began. And how it ends. This person who he once loved beyond all imagining, who came into his life like a tidal wave.

HER She wonders if she'll ever have children.

HIM Already she's a stranger, slipping away from him even as they walk side by side along this cold shingle beach. This was so important once. Dandelion heads blown by the wind. Don't go back.

HER Listen. Just listen.

FOR A MOMENT THE SOUND OF THE WIND, WAVES AND GULLS. THEN VERY LOUD, WAVES CRASHING. SOMETHING MUCH BIGGER THAN THEM. ELEMENTAL, TIMELESS. CHURCH BELLS CAN VERY FAINTLY BE HEARD IN THE DISTANCE.

HER Can you hear?
HIM I think we should go.

THEY REMAIN STANDING ON THE BEACH, ISOLATED IN THE OPEN SPACE, LISTENING AS THE SEASCAPE GRADUALLY FADES, LEAVING ONLY THE DISTANT UNDERWATER CHURCH BELLS, CLEAR NOW.

HER I think we should go.

THEY REMAIN STANDING UNTIL THEY TOO FADE WITH THE LIGHT.

Ends

ALSO BY JEREMY RAISON

THERESE RAQUIN
Five actors, (3m, 2f), optional chorus
Zola's classic tale given thrillingly theatrical treatment in a version that was acclaimed on its premiere at Glasgow Citizens Theatre in 2004. Therese is already married to her sickly cousin, Camille, when worldly Laurent is invited into her home. Murder brings Laurent and Therese together. It also tears them apart. Zola's novel has been much imitated, but never bettered.

WAKE ME IN THE MORNING
Three actors (2m, 1f)
The most famous actress in the world. The most powerful man. A brutal battle of the sexes leads to tragedy. Shades of Marilyn Monroe and J. F. Kennedy in this acclaimed stage play premiered in Glasgow at Oran Mor's A Play, A Pie and a Pint in 2014.

BRING ME SUNSHINE
Four actors (2m, 2f)
Eric isn't feeling well. He feels even worse when he realises Ernie is doing a funeral oration for him. Carol just wants her husband back, but something terrible has happened. Angie tries to help. A moving comedy about friendship, love and loss, featuring two men who may or may not be Eric Morecambe and Ernie Wise.

CANDYLAND
Three actors (2m, 1f)
Star has turned his back on his former wild life and retreated to an aircraft hangar in the middle of the Nevada desert. From now on he will live in peaceful seclusion with the woman he loves. Then City turns up uninvited. Soon secrets tumble out as it becomes clear that Star's idyllic isolation is not all it seems - and he'll do anything to protect himself.

THE SOUND OF MY VOICE
Two actors (1m, 1f)
Morris Magellan is a successful executive, but he has a problem. He is a chronic alcoholic. Ron Butlin's classic novel was adapted with great success for the Citizens Theatre and subsequently chosen by Made In Scotland to represent the best of Scottish work at the Edinburgh Festival, receiving 4 awards and seven 5 star reviews.